USING THIS BOOK

*Children learn to read by **reading**, but they need help to begin with.*

When you have read the story on the left-hand pages aloud to the child, go back to the beginning of the book and look at the pictures together.

Encourage children to read the sentences under the pictures. If they don't know a word, give them a chance to 'guess' what it is from the illustrations, before telling them.

There are more suggestions for helping children to learn to read in the *Parent/Teacher* booklet.

British Library Cataloguing in Publication Data

McCullagh, Sheila K.
    The Magician's party. — (Puddle Lane
    reading programme. Stage 3; 4)
    I. Title   II. Rowe, Gavin   III. Series
    428.6   PE1119
    ISBN 0-7214-0957-1

First edition

Published by Ladybird Books Ltd Loughborough Leicestershire UK
Ladybird Books Inc Lewiston Maine 04240 USA

The Magician's party

written by SHEILA McCULLAGH
illustrated by GAVIN ROWE

This book belongs to:

LYNSEY

Ladybird Books

It was firework night.
Sarah and Davy
were out in the lane.
They were making a guy.
They had a pair of old trousers
and a very old coat,
stuffed with straw.
They had an old bag
for the guy's head.
Two very old boots
lay beside them in the lane.

Sarah and Davy
were out in Puddle Lane.
They were making a guy.

5

Hari came out of his house,
and ran up the lane to the others.
He was carrying a pair
of old gloves.
"Would these do for his hands?"
he asked.

"Yes, they'd be just right," said Davy.

Hari came out of his house.
He ran up the lane
to Sarah and Davy.

"Let's get his boots on, and
then he's finished," said Sarah.
She stuffed the boots with straw,
and Hari and Davy tied them
on to the guy's legs.

Hari and Davy
put the boots
on the guy's legs.

Mr Gotobed came out of his house.
He was carrying a very old hat.
"Would you like this
for your guy?" he asked.
"You haven't got a hat for him,
have you?"

"No, we haven't, Mr Gotobed,"
said Sarah.
"Thank you very much.
It will look just right."
She put the hat
on the guy's head.

Mr Gotobed
came out of his house.
He had a very old hat.
Mr Gotobed asked,
"Would you like this
for your guy?"

There was a loud "Toot! Toot!"
from farther down the lane,
and Peter Puffle came out
of Mr Puffle's house.
He was blowing a tin horn.
When he saw the others,
he came running up the lane.
"Is that your guy?" he asked.

"Yes, he is," said Sarah.

"He's a good one this year,"
said Hari.

"He's the best we've ever made,"
said Davy.

Peter Puffle came up the lane.
Peter asked,
"Is that your guy?"

"Where's your bonfire?" asked Peter.

"We're not having a bonfire
this year," said Davy.

"Have you got any fireworks?"
asked Peter.
Sarah shook her head.
"Not this year," she said.

"No fireworks, Sarah?"
said Mr Gotobed.
"I wish I'd known that before."

"Have you got a bonfire?"
asked Peter.

"No," said Davy.

"Have you got any fireworks?"
asked Peter.

"No," said Sarah.

"I'm going to my grandad's,"
said Peter Puffle.
"He's built a big bonfire
in a field. He's got
a lot of fireworks, too."
Mr Puffle looked out of his door.
"Peter!" he called. "It's time to start."
Peter ran back to the house.
The others watched, as he went off
down the lane with Mr Puffle.
They felt rather sad.

Peter Puffle went off
down Puddle Lane.

"I know what we'll do,"
said Mr Gotobed.
"We'll have a party!
We'll have a party in Puddle Lane!"

"But we haven't any fireworks,"
said Davy.

"That doesn't matter," said Mr Gotobed.
"We can have a party, just the same."

"Aren't you going to bed,
Mr Gotobed?" asked Hari.

"Not today," said Mr Gotobed.

"We will have a party!"
said Mr Gotobed.
"We will have a party
in Puddle Lane!"

Mr Gotobed went off down the lane
to see Miss Baker.
He had only just gone, when
Mrs Pitter-Patter came up the lane.
"I hope you're not having fireworks
tonight, Sarah?" she said.
"All those nasty bangs!"

"We haven't any fireworks
this year," said Sarah.

"I'm very glad to hear it,"
said Mrs Pitter-Patter.
She went back down the lane.

Mrs Pitter-Patter
came up the lane.
She saw the guy.
"I hope you're not
having fireworks," she said.

The Magician lived in the house
at the end of Puddle Lane.
He had been out in his garden.
Nobody had seen him, but
he had heard every word.
"I think **I'll** go to this party,"
the Magician said to himself.
"Then there **will** be some fireworks!
But I'll tell the Griffle first."

The Magician was
in his garden.
''I will go to the party,''
he said.

The Griffle lived in
the Magician's garden.
He could vanish when
he wanted to, and
he was rather nervous.
He appeared, as soon as
the Magician called.
"Griffle," said the Magician,
"I wanted to warn you.
There's going to be a party
in Puddle Lane tonight.
And there will be fireworks."

The Magician called the Griffle.
The Griffle came.
''There will be fireworks
in Puddle Lane,''
said the Magician.

"I don't like fireworks,"
said the Griffle.
He looked very unhappy.
"I know you don't,"
said the Magician.
"None of the animals in the garden
like fireworks. They're frightened
of all the flashes and bangs.
I want you to go and tell them
to stay at home and hide.
Then they won't be frightened."

"I think I'll hide myself,"
said the Griffle.

"You can hide in my room,"
said the Magician. "But
tell the other animals first."

"I don't like fireworks,"
said the Griffle.

So the Griffle went round
to the other animals in the garden,
and warned them to stay
in their holes for the evening.
He left a note in the old tree
for the mice. (The Griffle
was afraid of mice, and
he didn't want to see them.
But he knew that Grandfather Mouse
had learnt to read, when he lived
in Mr Wideawake's toy shop.)

The Griffle left a note
for the mice.
He left it
in the old tree.

In Puddle Lane, everyone
was getting ready for the party.
Mr Gotobed opened his door, and
called to Davy to help him.
Between them, they carried a table
out into the lane.
Before very long, Miss Baker
came out of her house
with a big tray of cakes.
Hari ran home, and came back
with Gita, and a big jug,
full of lemonade.

Hari ran home.
He came back with Gita.

They were just going to begin,
when they heard music.
Someone was singing in Puddle Lane.
They couldn't see anyone, but
they could hear the words clearly:

There's magic in the air.
There's magic all around.
There's magic in the sunshine.
There's magic in the ground.
There's magic in the puddles.
There's magic in the rain,
when you belong to Candletown
and live in Puddle Lane.

Someone was singing
in Puddle Lane.

The gates at the end of the lane
opened, and the Magician came through.
"I thought you might like
some fireworks," he said.

"Fireworks!" cried Sarah and Davy.

"Fireworks!" cried Hari and Gita.

"Yes, fireworks," said the Magician.
"Watch!"
And he snapped his fingers.

The Magician
came into the lane.
''Fireworks!'' said the Magician.
And he snapped his fingers.

At once, the fireworks began.
There were red and green stars,
and whirls of fire.
There were big bangs.
There were blue and yellow stars,
and flashes of light.

The fireworks began.
There were red and green stars.
There were blue and yellow stars.

Mrs Pitter-Patter came rushing
up the lane.

"Whatever are you doing?" she cried.

"You said you weren't having fireworks!"

"Are you frightened of fireworks?"
asked the Magician.

"Of course not!" snapped Mrs Pitter-Patter.

"Then you won't mind a few, will you?"
said the Magician.

"It's firework night, you know."

A cracker went off in the lane.

"Stop it!" cried Mrs Pitter-Patter.

"You go home," said the Magician.

Mrs Pitter-Patter
came up the lane.
''You go home,''
said the Magician.

Mrs Pitter-Patter was very cross.
She was just going to say
that she wouldn't go home,
when she remembered that this
was a very great magician.
She tossed her head, and
went off down the lane.
When she got to her house,
she went in, and banged the door.
The Magician laughed.
He snapped his fingers, and
rockets shot up into the sky.

The Magician
snapped his fingers.

When at last the fireworks were over,
they had cakes and jellies and lemonade.
"We've never had fireworks
like this before," said Gita.

"It's the best firework night
we've ever had," said Davy.

"I expect the guy enjoyed it, too,"
said Sarah. "He's been able
to watch the fireworks, and
he hasn't been burnt on a bonfire!"

Notes for the parent/teacher

Turn back to the beginning, and print the child's name in the space on the title page, using ordinary, not capital letters.

Now go through the book again. Look at each picture and talk about it. Point to the caption below, and read it aloud yourself.

Run your finger along under the words as you read, so that the child learns that reading goes from left to right.

Encourage the child to read the words under the illustrations. Don't rush in with the word before he/she has had time to think, but don't leave him/her struggling.

Read this story as often as the child likes hearing it. The more opportunities he/she has of looking at the illustrations and **reading** the captions with you, the more he/she will come to recognise the words.

If you have several books, let the child choose which story he/she would like.

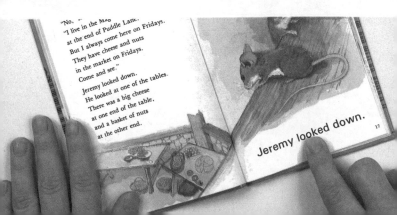

When the fireworks were over,
they had a party
in Puddle Lane.